Wonderfully
Made

Written and Illustrated by Meggan A. MacKenzie

AuthorHouse™
1663 Liberty Drive
Bloomington, IN 47403
www.authorhouse.com
Phone: 1 (800) 839-8640

Published by AuthorHouse 06/22/2018

ISBN: 978-1-5462-4399-1 (SC)
ISBN: 978-1-5462-4400-4 (e)
ISBN: 978-1-5462-4398-4 (hc)

Print information available on the last page.

authorHOUSE®

This book is dedicated to my children Madelynn and Samuel, and to my Goddaughter Magnolia. May you always feel the love of God and know just how fearfully and wonderfully you were made.

In a quiet and peaceful moment, one that doesn't come along very often or is soon to be forgotten, a mother and her child snuggled in the sunshine. The leaves danced gently with the wind while the sun's rays played peek-a-boo through the tops of the trees. The birds chirped, the frogs sang, and the bees went about their business. The whole earth seemed to breathe with life. The mother smiled while her child looked up at her lovingly, and then down again at her hands.

"Momma?"

"Yes Monkey?"

"Why did God give me hands?"

The mother paused. The mother prayed. The mother answered as God whispered.

"God gave you hands so that you could help people. When we do this we are serving and loving God."

Serve the Lord with gladness; Come before Him with joyful singing.
~ Psalm 100:2

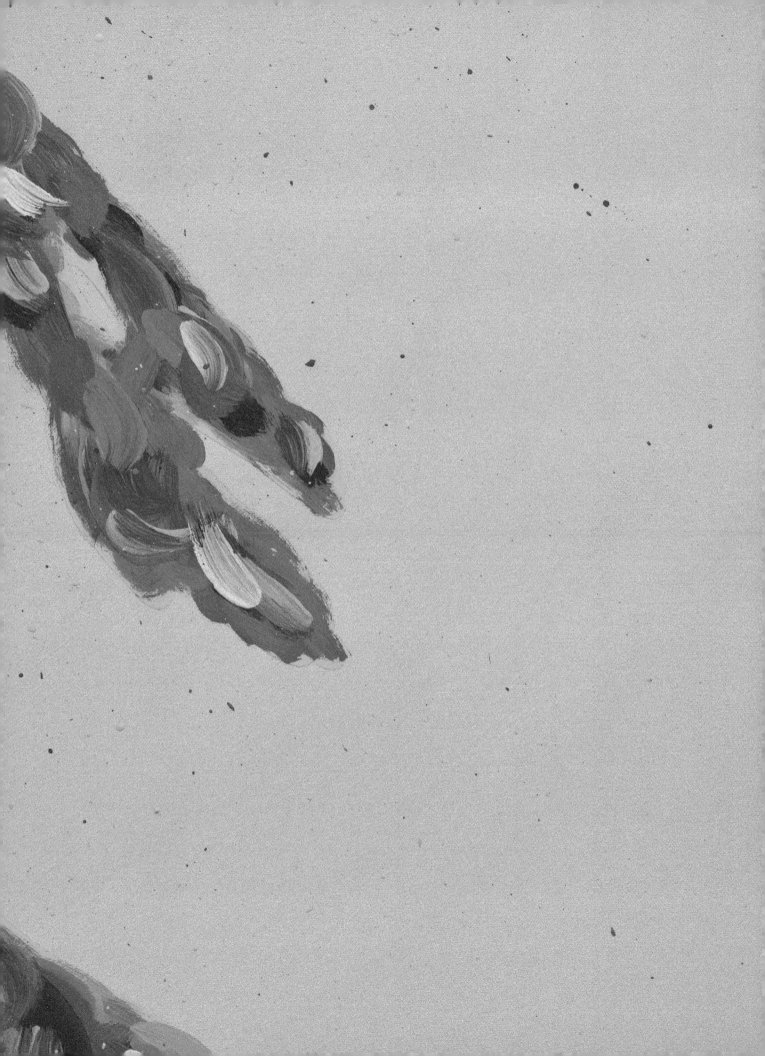

"Momma?"

"Yes Peanut?"

"Why did God give me feet?"

The mother paused. The mother prayed. The mother answered as God whispered.

"God gave you feet so that you could follow Jesus. To trust in Him wherever He may lead you."

Your word is a lamp for my feet and a light to my path. ~ Psalm 119:105

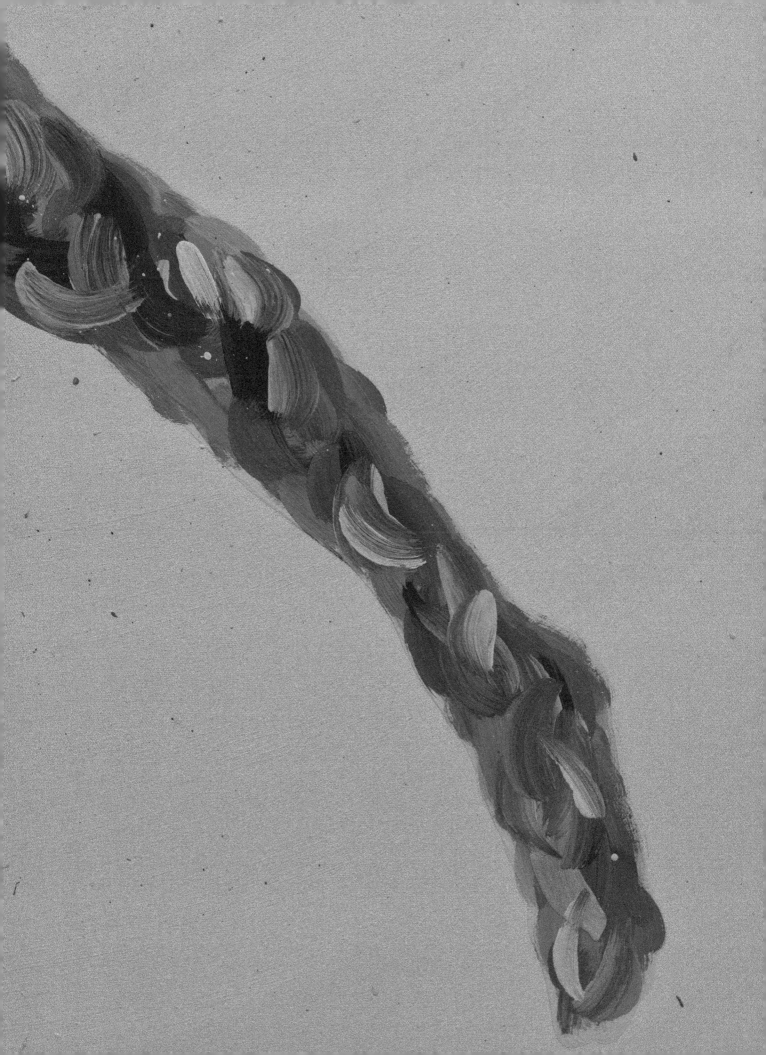

"Momma?"

"Yes My Love?"

"Why did God give me eyes?"

The mother paused. The mother prayed. The mother answered as God whispered.

"God gave you eyes so that you could see His creation. To see the beauty and wonder in all things both great and small, including you."

God looked over everything he had made; it was so good, so very good! ~ Genesis 1:31

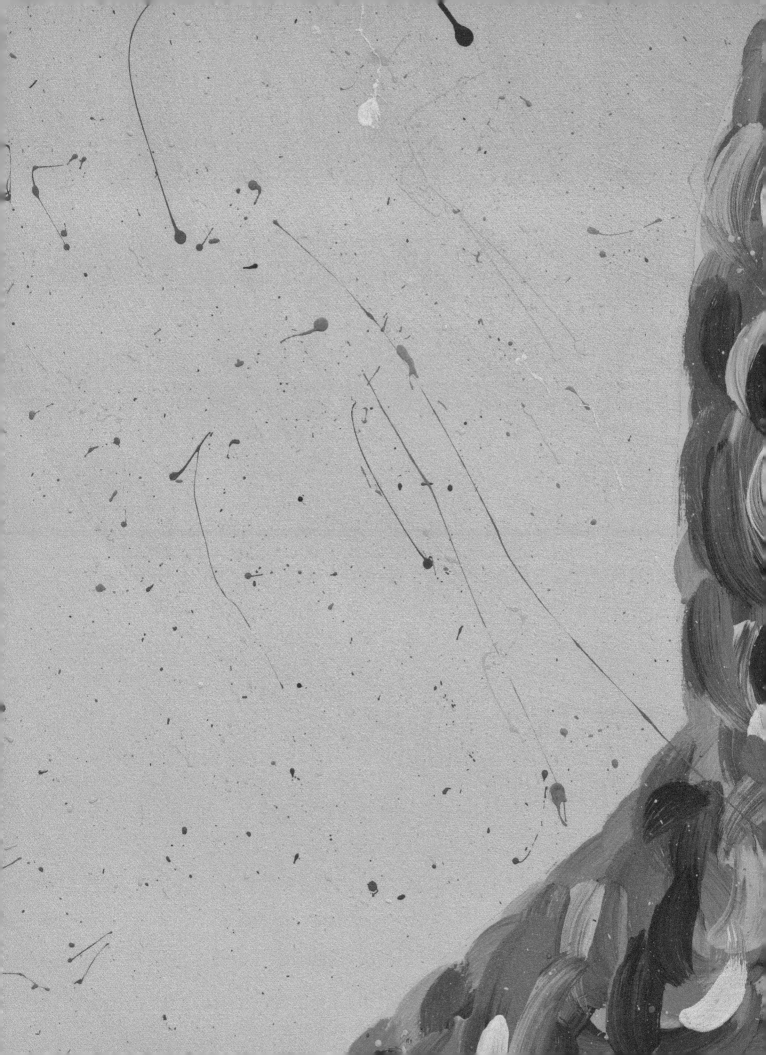

"Momma?"

"Yes Sunshine?"

"Why did God give me ears?"

The mother paused. The mother prayed. The mother answered as God whispered.

"God gave you ears so that you could hear Him when He talks to you. To learn all about Him and what He wants for your life."

Therefore everyone who hears these words of mine and puts them into practice is like a wise man who built his house on the rock.
~ Matthew 7:24

"Momma?"

"Yes Pumpkin?"

"Why did God give me a mouth?"

The mother paused. The mother prayed. The mother answered as God whispered.

"God gave you a mouth so that you could tell others about Him and His son Jesus. He wants us to speak His truth."

For the word of the Lord is right and true; he is faithful in all he does. ~ Psalm 33:4

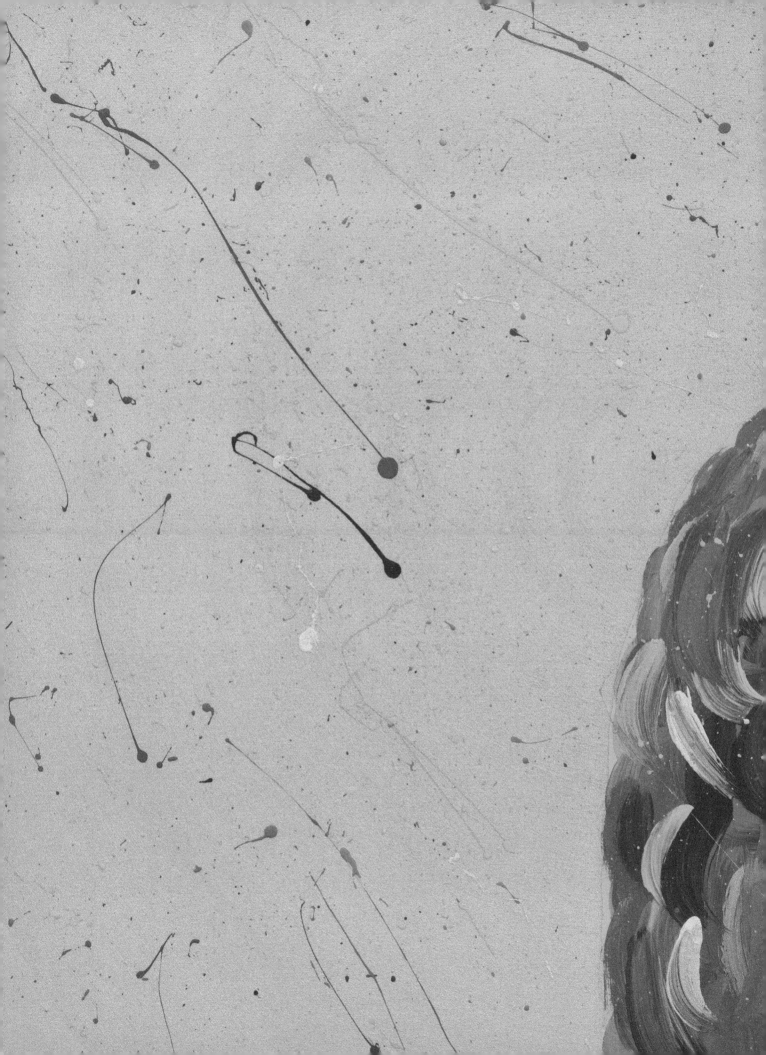

"Momma?"

"Yes Cutie Pie?"

"Why did God give me shoulders?"

The mother paused. The mother prayed. The mother answered as God whispered.

"God gave you shoulders so that you could feel the weight of your problems. He always wants us to go to Him, especially when we need help."

God is our refuge and strength, an ever-present help in time of trouble. ~ Psalm 46:1

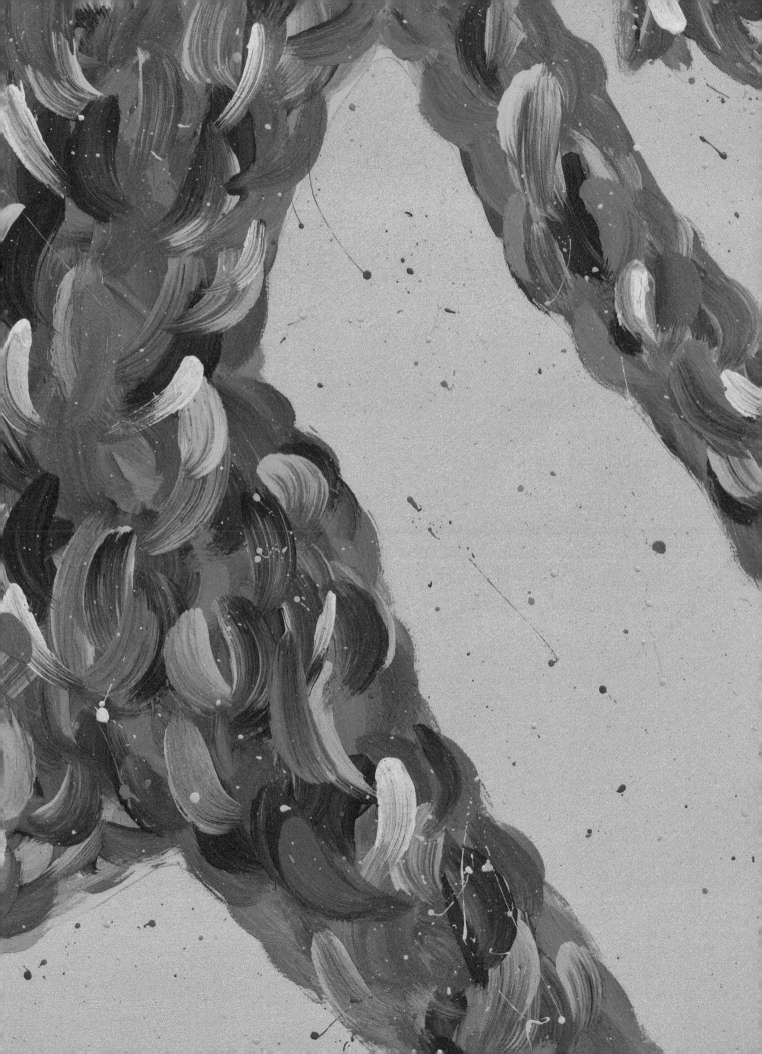

"Momma?"

"Yes Sweet Pea?"

"Why did God give me a heart?"

The mother paused. The mother prayed. The mother answered as God whispered.

"God gave you a heart so that you could learn how to love like He loves us. He wants us to learn the true meaning of forgiveness, kindness, and grace."

God is Love. Whoever lives in love lives in God, and God in them.
~ 1 John 4:16

"Momma?"

"Yes Wee One?"

"Why did God give me a back?"

The mother paused. The mother prayed. The mother answered as God whispered.

"God gave you a back and a backbone so that you could stand up for yourself and others. Sometimes life will be hard and God wants you to be strong in your faith.

The Lord is on my side; I will not fear. ~ Psalm 118:6.

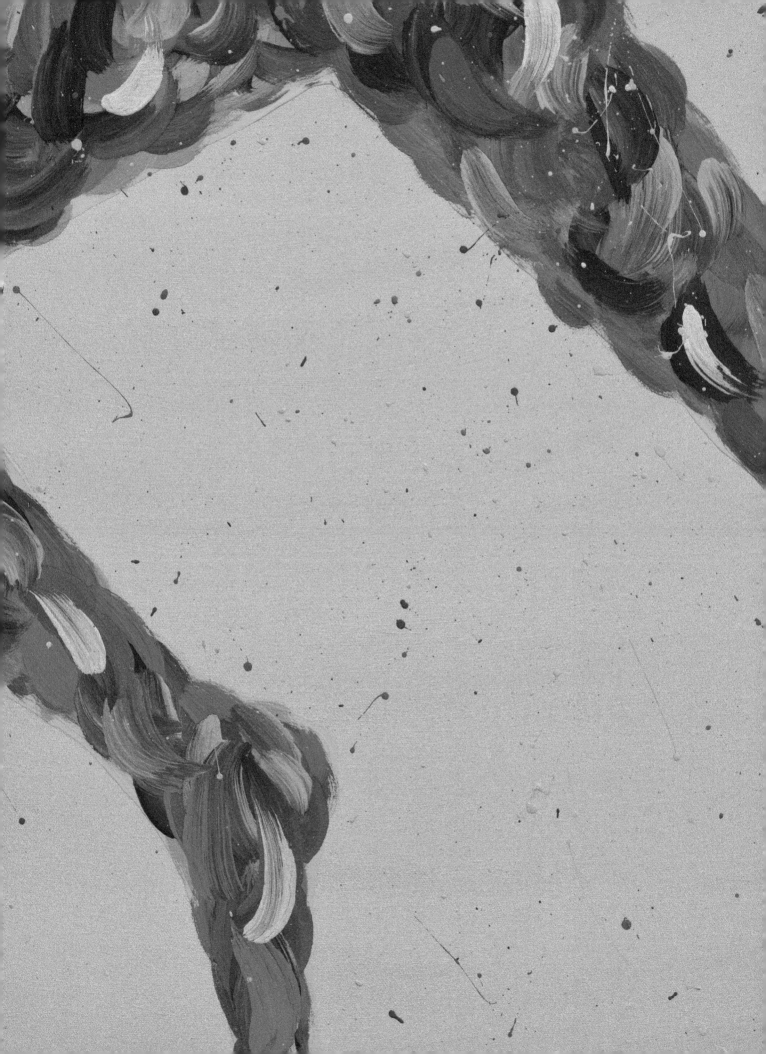

"Momma?"

"Yes Love Bug?"

"Why did God give me knees?"

The mother paused. The mother prayed. The mother answered as God whispered.

"God gave you knees so that you could kneel before Him and pray. God loves when we talk to him and say thank you."

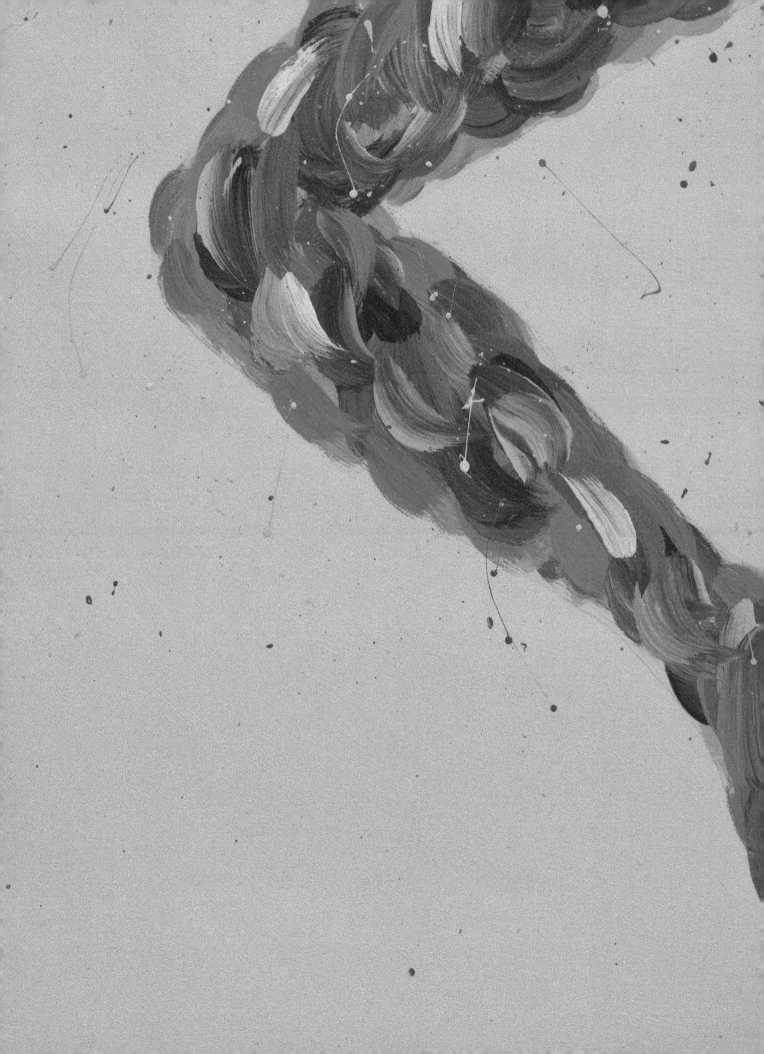

"Momma?"

"Yes Dear One?"

".....Why did God make me?"

The mother paused..... The mother prayed.... The mother answered as God whispered.

"...God made you uniquely you, every part of you. From the tips of your hair to the soles of your feet. Your inside. Your outside. Your heart, soul, and spirit. All of you is from God and from God alone. You are His masterpiece and making you gave Him great joy. God made you with certain gifts so that you could use those gifts to shine His light into the world. He wants you to show everyone His love so that they can come to know Him too. To know the Father, the Son, and the Holy Spirit. My Dear One...*that is why God made you.*"

I praise you because I am fearfully and wonderfully made. ~ Psalm 139:14

CPSIA information can be obtained
at www.ICGtesting.com
Printed in the USA
LVHW07*1932140918
590206LV00002B/2/P